DIGITAL PIONEERS

EMPOWERING KIDS IN THE TECH WORLD

DR. MINAKSHI BANSAL

Made with ♥ on the Notion Press Platform
www.notionpress.com

DEDICATION

To my children, the original digital pioneers, who inspire me every day with their curiosity, creativity, and boundless potential. May you always embrace the joy of learning, use your tech skills for good, and never stop exploring the endless possibilities of the digital world.

♡♡♡

Contents

Contents

Contents

Prayer

"Om Bhadram Karnebhih Shrinuyama Devah

Bhadram Pashyemakshabhiryajatrah

Sthirairangais Tushtuvamsastanubhih

Vyashema Devahitam Yadayuh

Svasti Na Indro Vriddhashravah

Svasti Nah Pusha Vishwavedah

Svasti Nastarkshyo Arishtanemih

Svasti No Brihaspatir Dadhatu

Om Shantih Shantih Shantih"

This mantra is a prayer for universal well-being, invoking the blessings of various deities for protection, health, and happiness. It emphasizes the importance of experiencing the auspicious through all senses and living a life aligned with divine purpose. The repetition of "Shantih" at the end signifies a deep desire for peace in the individual, the environment, and the universe at large. This mantra is often recited as a prayer for peace, prosperity, and the physical and spiritual well-being of all beings.

ᐁᐁᐁ

About The Author

This book represents the culmination of extensive research and meticulous analysis, incorporating a diverse range of sources, including numerous books, scholarly studies, and personal experiences. Additionally, I have scoured various websites to gather relevant information and data essential for the compilation of this work. I have taken every precaution to ensure the accuracy of the information presented and have diligently cited all sources to acknowledge their contributions.

From her earliest days, Minakshi was distinguished by an insatiable appetite for reading. Her literary universe was inhabited by characters and narratives that spanned ethical tales, motivational and inspirational stories, and the mythic parables imbued with life lessons. This voracious reading habit was not merely for personal edification but was driven by a desire to distill and disseminate the essence of these narratives to foster the development of students and peers alike. She was particularly captivated by the lives and teachings of historical figures and spiritual leaders such as Adi Shankaracharya, Swami Vivekananda, Dr. APJ Abdul Kalam, Mahamana Pandit Madan Mohan Malviya, Mahatma Gandhi, Sardar Vallabhai Patel, and Vinoba Bhave, among others. Their philosophies and life stories fueled her ambition to embody their ideals of resilience, selflessness, and relentless pursuit of knowledge.

Dr. Minakshi's academic and practical engagement with psychology has been equally noteworthy. As a research scholar, her focus has been on exploring the intricate tapestry of the human psyche, aiming to unlock the potential for psychological well-being and societal harmony. Her scholarly work is complemented by her active involvement in social work, where she employs her academic insights to make tangible differences in the lives of the underprivileged. Her endeavours in social work are characterized by an innovative approach that combines traditional wisdom with contemporary psychological practices to address the multifaceted challenges faced by these communities.

Her artistic talents, another facet of her diverse capabilities, are not merely a personal passion but also serve as a medium through which she communicates and connects with others. Her art, rich in symbolism and emotional depth, reflects her philosophical inquiries and social concerns, offering viewers a glimpse into the breadth of her intellect and the depth of her compassion.

In addition to her contributions to the arts and social sciences, Dr. Minakshi has embraced the healing arts of Pranic Healing, mastering the techniques developed by Master Choa Kok Sui. This practice, which focuses on the manipulation of Prana or life energy to heal the body and aura, has been both a personal journey of discovery and a means through which she extends her healing touch to others. Her proficiency in Pranic Healing is complemented by her advocacy and teaching of various forms of meditation aimed at rejuvenation, personal betterment, and the cultivation of harmony within individuals and communities alike.

Dr. Minakshi's life is a narrative of relentless pursuit, not just of personal achievement but of the upliftment and empowerment of society at large. Her diverse interests and talents—spanning the arts, literature, psychology, and the healing practices—converge on a singular path of service. She embodies the spirit of the luminaries who inspired her, channelling their legacy through her actions and teachings. Through her books, art, and social initiatives, she continues to inspire a new generation to embark on their own journeys of self-discovery, resilience, and altruism.

Her commitment to social betterment, particularly her focus on uplifting underprivileged children, reflects a deep understanding of the transformative potential of education and personal development. By integrating her knowledge of psychology, her artistic sensibilities, and her healing practices, Dr. Bansal has developed a holistic approach to social work that addresses both the immediate needs and the long-term well-being of the communities she serves.

As an author, Dr. Minakshi's writings offer a blend of inspirational insights, practical wisdom, and reflective contemplations drawn from her extensive reading and life experiences. Her books serve as a guide for those seeking to navigate the complexities of life with grace, resilience, and purpose. Through her narratives, she extends an invitation to her readers to explore the depths of their own potential and to contribute meaningfully to the collective well-being of society.

In Dr. Minakshi Bansal, we find a remarkable synthesis of the artist, the scholar, the healer, and the social activist. Her life's work stands as a beacon of hope and a source of inspiration for individuals seeking to make a difference in the world. Her story is a compelling reminder of the power of individual action, rooted in compassion and driven by a profound commitment to the betterment of humanity. Dr. Minakshi's legacy is not just in the tangible outcomes of her efforts but in the enduring spirit of inquiry, empathy, and service that she embodies.

ॐॐॐ

Preface

As a mom navigating the uncharted waters of the digital age, I often found myself grappling with a mix of excitement and apprehension. The world my children were growing up in was vastly different from the one I knew as a child. Technology was no longer a novelty; it was an integral part of their lives, shaping how they learned, played, and interacted with the world.

I marveled at their natural aptitude for technology, their ability to intuitively navigate touchscreens and master complex apps at a young age. But I also worried about the potential pitfalls of this digital immersion. Would excessive screen time hinder their development? Would they become overly reliant on technology, losing touch with the real world? And how could I ensure they were using technology safely and responsibly?

These questions led me on a journey of exploration and discovery. I sought out resources, talked to experts, and most importantly, observed my own children as they interacted with technology. What I discovered was a world of possibilities, a landscape filled with opportunities for learning, creativity, and growth.

In this book, I share my experiences and insights, offering a practical guide for parents who, like me, want to empower their children to thrive in the digital age. This is not a book about banning technology or demonizing screen time. It's about embracing technology as a tool for learning, creativity, and connection, while also setting healthy boundaries and fostering responsible digital habits.

You'll find a wealth of information on topics ranging from coding and robotics to digital citizenship and online safety. You'll discover fun and engaging activities that can transform screen time into learning adventures, and you'll learn how to create a tech-friendly home environment that encourages exploration and experimentation. But most importantly, you'll gain the confidence and knowledge you need to raise tech-savvy kids who are prepared for the future.

This book is not just for parents of young children. It's for anyone who wants to understand the impact of technology on children's lives and empower them to navigate the digital world with confidence and creativity. Whether you're a parent, grandparent, educator, or mentor, this book will provide you with valuable insights and practical strategies for raising the next generation of digital pioneers.

My hope is that this book will inspire you to see technology not as a threat, but as a tool for empowerment. I believe that every child has the potential to be a digital creator, an innovator, and a problem solver. By fostering their curiosity, nurturing their creativity, and guiding them towards responsible tech use, we can empower them to shape a brighter future for themselves and for the world.

Dr. Minakshi Bansal
Social Activist
Ahmedabad, Gujarat, Bharat

ᐅᐅᐅ

ONE

RAISE TECH-SAVVY KIDS: A MOM'S GUIDE TO CODING, CREATIVITY & CONFIDENCE.

In today's rapidly evolving digital landscape, the ability to navigate and understand technology is no longer a luxury, but a necessity. As a mom, I've witnessed firsthand the transformative power of technology in my children's lives. It's been a journey of discovery, excitement, and occasional challenges, but ultimately, one that has filled me with hope for the future. This guide is born from my personal experiences and the insights I've gained along the way. It's a testament to the belief that every child, regardless of background or gender, can become a confident digital pioneer.

Our children are growing up in a world where technology is seamlessly integrated into every aspect of daily life. From smartphones and tablets to smart homes and artificial intelligence, the digital age is here to stay. As parents, it's our responsibility to equip our children with the skills they need to thrive in this ever-changing environment. But it's not just about teaching them how to use the latest gadgets; it's about fostering a deep understanding of how technology works, sparking their curiosity, and nurturing their creativity.

Coding, often considered the language of the future, is an excellent starting point for this journey. It's not just about learning to write lines of code; it's about developing computational thinking skills that can be applied to a wide range of problems. Coding teaches children to break down complex tasks into smaller, more manageable steps, to think logically, and to persevere in the face of challenges. It empowers them to become creators, not just consumers, of technology.

There are countless resources available to help parents introduce coding to their children, from age-appropriate apps and games to online courses and coding camps. The key is to start early and make it fun. Look for activities that spark your child's interest and encourage them to explore at their own pace. Remember, the goal is to ignite a passion for learning, not to turn them into overnight experts.

Creativity is another crucial component of tech-savviness. In a world where artificial intelligence is becoming increasingly sophisticated, it's our children's unique ability to think outside the box that will set them apart. Encourage them to experiment with different technologies, to explore their artistic talents through digital media, and to find innovative solutions to real-world problems.

Building confidence is equally important. In a society that often stereotypes girls and young women as being less interested or capable in STEM fields, it's crucial to provide them with the support and encouragement they need to break down those barriers. Celebrate their achievements, big and small, and remind them that their potential is limitless.

As a mom, I've seen firsthand how technology can empower my children. My daughter, once hesitant to try anything new, has blossomed into a confident coder who loves creating her own games and animations. My son, initially intimidated by complex concepts, now approaches challenges with a newfound sense of curiosity and determination.

Empowering our children in the tech world is not just about preparing them for future careers; it's about giving them the tools they need to navigate an increasingly complex world with confidence and resilience. It's about fostering a lifelong love of learning and a passion for innovation.

This guide is not a one-size-fits-all solution. Every child is unique, with their own interests, strengths, and learning styles. It's important to tailor your approach to your child's individual needs and to be patient and supportive throughout their journey.

The digital age presents both challenges and opportunities for our children. As parents, it's our responsibility to help them navigate this new frontier with wisdom and confidence. By fostering their curiosity, nurturing their creativity, and building their confidence, we can empower them to become the digital pioneers of tomorrow.

Remember, this is a journey, not a destination. The tech world is constantly evolving, and so are our children. The most important thing is to foster a love of learning and a willingness to embrace new challenges. With our guidance and support, our children can achieve anything they set their minds to.

ppp

"In a world overflowing with digital distractions, we have the power to ignite our children's curiosity. Let's turn screen time into a launchpad for creativity, where coding isn't just a language, but a superpower."

TWO

SCREEN TIME REVOLUTION: NURTURING YOUNG INNOVATORS IN A DIGITAL AGE.

The phrase "screen time" often evokes a sense of unease among parents. Visions of children glued to their devices, passively consuming content, and neglecting the "real world" can be disheartening. However, I believe it's time to reframe our perspective. In this digital age, screens are not simply entertainment portals; they are powerful tools that can be harnessed to nurture young innovators.

The digital world is teeming with opportunities for learning, creation, and connection. From coding games and educational apps to online communities and collaborative projects, the possibilities are endless. As parents, it's our responsibility to guide our children through this landscape, helping them discover the hidden gems and avoiding the pitfalls. It's about embracing the screen time revolution and transforming it into a catalyst for growth.

Imagine a child who spends hours engrossed in a video game. At first glance, it might seem like wasted time. But what if that game sparked their interest in coding? What if it inspired them to create their own levels or modifications? Suddenly, screen time becomes a gateway to a new world of possibilities. By encouraging children to explore their interests and passions through technology, we can ignite a spark of creativity that could lead to a lifelong love of learning.

Of course, not all screen time is created equal. Mindless scrolling through social media or binge-watching videos can be detrimental to a child's development. The key is to strike a balance between passive consumption and active engagement. Encourage your children to use technology as a tool for creation, not just consumption.

This can be as simple as introducing them to age-appropriate coding apps that teach them the basics of programming, or encouraging them to use video editing software to create their own movies. Even something as seemingly mundane as playing Minecraft can foster creativity and problem-solving skills.

Beyond individual exploration, the digital age offers a wealth of opportunities for collaboration and connection. Online communities can be a haven for young innovators, providing a space to share ideas, learn from others, and collaborate on projects. Encourage your child to join online forums or groups related to their interests, or to participate in virtual workshops and competitions.

However, it's important to remember that the digital world can also be a dangerous place. Cyberbullying, online predators, and exposure to inappropriate content are real risks that we must be aware of. As parents, it's crucial to have open and honest conversations with our children about online safety, to set clear boundaries and expectations, and to monitor their online activity.

The screen time revolution is not just about individual children; it's about shaping the future of our society. By empowering our children to become digital creators and innovators, we are investing in a brighter future. We are nurturing a generation that is not afraid to embrace new technologies, to challenge the status quo, and to create a world that is more connected, more innovative, and more equitable.

The potential of the digital age is vast, but it's up to us to ensure that our children are equipped to navigate it safely and responsibly. By embracing the screen time revolution, we can transform a source of anxiety into a source of empowerment. We can raise a generation of digital pioneers who are not just consumers of technology, but creators of a better tomorrow.

This is not a call to abandon the real world in favor of the digital one. Rather, it's a call to embrace the potential of both. Encourage your children to balance their screen time with outdoor play, face-to-face interactions, and other activities that promote their physical and mental well-being.

The key is to view technology as a tool, not a crutch. By teaching our children how to use technology responsibly and creatively, we can unlock a world of possibilities. We can empower them to become the innovators, entrepreneurs, and leaders of tomorrow. The screen time revolution is here to stay, and it's up to us to make the most of it.

ppp

"The digital age isn't a threat; it's an invitation. An invitation for our kids to become architects of their own virtual worlds, where innovation isn't just encouraged, it's expected."

THREE

CODE LIKE A GIRL: INSPIRING THE NEXT GENERATION OF FEMALE TECH LEADERS.

The tech world, with its relentless innovation and limitless possibilities, has long been a male-dominated domain. However, a quiet revolution is underway. A new generation of girls and young women are stepping up to challenge the status quo, armed with a passion for technology and a drive to make their mark on the world. This movement, often encapsulated by the phrase "Code Like a Girl," is about more than just learning to program; it's about breaking down stereotypes, empowering girls to pursue their dreams, and building a more inclusive and equitable tech industry.

From a young age, girls are often bombarded with messages that subtly (and sometimes not so subtly) discourage them from pursuing interests in STEM fields. They are told that boys are better at math and science, that technology is a "boy's thing," and that their talents lie elsewhere. These stereotypes can be incredibly damaging, instilling a sense of self-doubt and limiting girls' aspirations.

However, the reality is quite different. Girls are just as capable as boys when it comes to technology. In fact, research has shown that girls often outperform boys in early math and science courses. The problem is not a lack of ability, but a lack of encouragement and opportunity.

The "Code Like a Girl" movement seeks to address this issue by providing girls with the resources and support they need to thrive in the tech world. This includes everything from coding workshops and summer camps to mentorship programs and online communities. By creating a safe and supportive environment where girls can learn and explore their interests, we can help them build the confidence and skills they need to succeed.

The impact of this movement is already being felt. More and more girls are choosing to study computer science and other STEM subjects in college. They are starting their own tech companies, developing innovative products, and leading teams of talented engineers and designers. These young women are not just breaking glass ceilings; they are shattering them.

But the work is far from over. The tech industry still has a long way to go in terms of diversity and inclusion. Women remain underrepresented in leadership positions, and they often face discrimination and harassment in the workplace. Changing this culture will require a concerted effort from everyone involved, from parents and educators to tech companies and policymakers.

One of the most powerful ways to inspire the next generation of female tech leaders is to provide them with role models. By showcasing the achievements of successful women in tech, we can show girls that they too can achieve their dreams. This can be as simple as sharing stories of inspiring women on social media, inviting female tech professionals to speak at schools and community events, or highlighting the contributions of women in tech history.

Mentorship programs can also play a crucial role in empowering girls in tech. By pairing young girls with experienced mentors who can offer guidance, support, and encouragement, we can help them navigate the challenges they may face and build the skills they need to succeed.

It's also important to create a culture of inclusivity in the tech world. This means creating workplaces where everyone feels valued and respected, regardless of their gender, race, ethnicity, or sexual orientation. It means celebrating diversity and recognizing that different perspectives can lead to better solutions.

The "Code Like a Girl" movement is not just about getting more girls into tech; it's about creating a more equitable and inclusive industry for everyone. By empowering girls to pursue their dreams, we can unlock a wealth of untapped talent and creativity. We can build a tech world that is more representative of the diversity of our society, and we can create a better future for all.

This is a call to action for all of us. Parents, educators, tech companies, and policymakers all have a role to play in inspiring the next generation of female tech leaders. By working together, we can create a world where every girl has the opportunity to reach her full potential and make her mark on the world.

ᔭᔭᔭ

*"Girls, don't let anyone tell you tech isn't for you.
Code like a girl, build like a girl, dream like a girl,
and shatter every stereotype that dares to limit
your potential."*

FOUR

Unleash Their Potential: Fun & Easy Projects for Future Tech Stars.

In the heart of every child lies a spark of curiosity, a yearning to explore, and a boundless potential waiting to be unleashed. As parents and educators, we have the incredible opportunity to nurture this potential, especially in the realm of technology. The digital age offers a playground of possibilities for young minds to learn, create, and innovate. By engaging children in fun and easy tech projects, we can ignite their passion for technology, foster essential skills, and set them on a path towards becoming future tech stars.

The beauty of these projects lies in their accessibility. They don't require expensive equipment or advanced knowledge. With just a few simple tools and a sprinkle of creativity, children can embark on exciting adventures in the world of technology. Let's explore some of these projects that can unleash their potential:

1. Coding Adventures: Coding is the language of the digital world, and introducing children to it at an early age can open up a world of possibilities. Start with visual coding platforms like Scratch or Blockly, where children can drag and drop blocks to create animations, games, and interactive stories. As they gain confidence, they can transition to text-based coding languages like Python or JavaScript. Coding not only teaches children how to create digital experiences but also fosters problem-solving, logical thinking, and computational skills.

2. Robotics Exploration: Robotics is a fascinating field that combines engineering, coding, and creativity. Many affordable robotics kits are available that allow children to build and program their own robots. They can design robots to perform various tasks, such as navigating mazes, following lines, or even playing soccer. Robotics projects teach children about mechanics, electronics, and programming, while also encouraging teamwork and collaboration.

3. Game Design Challenges: Who doesn't love playing games? But have you ever considered creating your own? Game design is a fantastic way to unleash creativity and learn about game mechanics, storytelling, and user experience. Children can use game design platforms like Roblox or GameMaker to build their own virtual worlds and characters. They can create puzzles, challenges, and storylines, all while developing their design and coding skills.

4. 3D Printing Creations: 3D printing is revolutionizing the way we create objects. Children can use 3D modeling software like Tinkercad to design their own toys, gadgets, or even functional tools. They can then print their creations using a 3D printer, turning their digital designs into tangible objects. 3D printing projects

nurture spatial reasoning, design thinking, and problem-solving skills.

5. Electronics Experiments: Electronics is the backbone of modern technology, and experimenting with circuits and components can be a thrilling experience for children. Start with simple projects like building a flashlight or a buzzer using batteries, wires, and LEDs. As they progress, they can explore more complex circuits and even build their own electronic gadgets. Electronics projects teach children about electricity, circuits, and soldering, while also fostering curiosity and a sense of accomplishment.

6. App Development Adventures: Mobile apps are ubiquitous in our daily lives, and children can learn to create their own with user-friendly app development platforms like App Inventor or Thunkable. They can design apps to solve problems, share information, or even create games. App development projects teach children about user interface design, data management, and programming logic.

7. Website Wonders: Websites are the digital storefronts of the internet, and children can learn to build their own using platforms like WordPress or Wix. They can create websites to showcase their hobbies, share their writing, or even start a small online business. Website projects teach children about web design, content creation, and online marketing.

8. Digital Storytelling Delights: Storytelling is a fundamental human activity, and technology offers exciting new ways to tell stories. Children can use animation software like Powtoon or Vyond to create animated videos, or they can use digital storytelling platforms like Storybird to write and illustrate their own stories. Digital storytelling projects encourage creativity, communication, and critical thinking.

The key to unleashing children's potential in the tech world is to make learning fun and engaging. Let them choose projects that spark their interest, encourage them to experiment and explore, and celebrate their successes. Remember, it's not about creating perfect products; it's about nurturing a lifelong love of learning and a passion for technology.

As parents and educators, we have a responsibility to equip our children with the skills they need to thrive in the digital age. By engaging them in fun and easy tech projects, we can unleash their potential, foster their creativity, and empower them to become the future tech stars of tomorrow. The possibilities are endless, and the journey is just beginning.

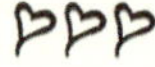

"Unleashing a child's potential is like planting a seed. With the right tools, guidance, and a sprinkle of tech magic, watch them blossom into the innovators of tomorrow."

"Learning doesn't have to be confined to textbooks and classrooms. In the digital realm, every click, every line of code, every pixel crafted is a step towards a brighter future."

FIVE

FROM GAMING TO CODING: TURN SCREEN TIME INTO LEARNING ADVENTURES.

The allure of video games is undeniable, especially for children. Hours can easily slip by as they immerse themselves in fantastical worlds, solve puzzles, and conquer challenges. While this often sparks concern among parents worried about excessive screen time, it also presents a unique opportunity. The same engagement and enthusiasm children have for gaming can be harnessed and redirected towards a more educational and enriching pursuit: coding.

At first glance, gaming and coding might seem worlds apart. One is about entertainment and leisure, the other about logic and problem-solving. However, a closer look reveals a surprising synergy between the two. Many popular video games incorporate elements of coding, whether it's the complex algorithms that govern the game's mechanics or the creative design of its characters and environments. By tapping into children's existing interest in gaming, we can introduce them to the world of coding in a way that is both fun and engaging.

Consider the popular game Minecraft. While seemingly a simple world-building game, it offers a powerful introduction to coding concepts. Players can use command blocks to create custom game mechanics, automate tasks, and even build complex structures. This hands-on experience teaches them the basics of programming logic, such as loops, conditional statements, and variables. Suddenly, the game is no longer just about survival and exploration; it's a platform for creativity and experimentation.

Another example is the educational game Lightbot. This puzzle game challenges players to guide a robot through a series of mazes by programming its movements. As they progress, they encounter increasingly complex challenges that require them to think critically and apply coding concepts. In this way, Lightbot seamlessly blends entertainment with education, turning screen time into a valuable learning experience.

The transition from gaming to coding doesn't have to be abrupt. Many games offer modding tools that allow players to modify existing games or create their own levels. This can be an excellent starting point for children interested in coding. By experimenting with these tools, they can gain a basic understanding of how games are made and develop their coding skills in a familiar and enjoyable context.

Beyond individual games, there are numerous online resources and communities dedicated to teaching children how to code through games. Platforms like CodeCombat and Tynker offer interactive coding courses that use game-like elements to engage learners.

Children can earn rewards, level up, and compete with their peers, all while learning valuable coding skills. These platforms not only make learning fun but also foster a sense of community and collaboration.

Of course, the transition from gaming to coding is not always seamless. Some children might be reluctant to give up their favorite games in favor of coding. In such cases, it's important to be patient and understanding. Start by introducing coding in small doses, perhaps by suggesting a coding game or app that aligns with their interests. Encourage them to explore coding concepts at their own pace, and celebrate their successes along the way.

It's also important to emphasize that coding is not just about creating games. It's a skill that can be applied to a wide range of fields, from robotics and artificial intelligence to web development and data science. By helping children understand the broader applications of coding, we can broaden their horizons and inspire them to pursue a variety of career paths.

The transition from gaming to coding is more than just a shift in activities; it's a mindset shift. It's about empowering children to become creators, not just consumers of technology. By nurturing their curiosity, creativity, and problem-solving skills, we can equip them with the tools they need to thrive in the digital age.

The future belongs to those who can code. By turning screen time into learning adventures, we can prepare our children for this future and empower them to shape it.

ᐳᐳᐳ

"Gaming isn't just about fun; it's a portal to a world of possibilities. Let's transform those button-mashing hours into coding adventures, where problem-solving is the ultimate quest."

SIX

DIGITAL PARENTING MADE EASY: A PRACTICAL GUIDE FOR MODERN FAMILIES.

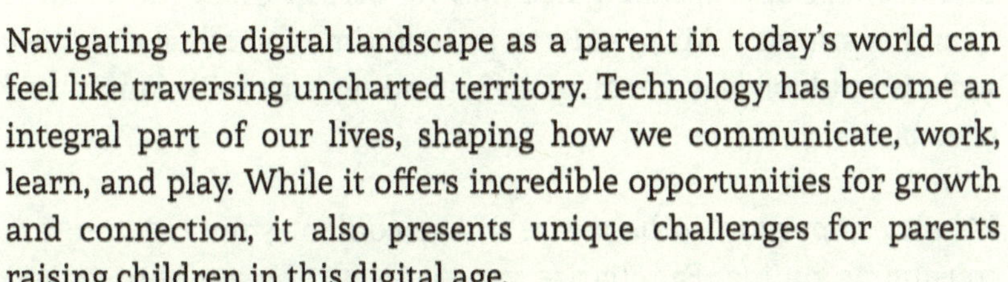

Navigating the digital landscape as a parent in today's world can feel like traversing uncharted territory. Technology has become an integral part of our lives, shaping how we communicate, work, learn, and play. While it offers incredible opportunities for growth and connection, it also presents unique challenges for parents raising children in this digital age.

The goal of this guide is to simplify the complex world of digital parenting, providing practical strategies and insights to help modern families thrive in the digital age.

First and foremost, it's important to acknowledge that technology is here to stay. Rather than fearing or resisting it, we must embrace it as a tool that can enrich our children's lives.

This means educating ourselves about the various technologies our children are using, understanding their potential benefits and risks, and setting clear boundaries and expectations.

One of the most crucial aspects of digital parenting is open communication. Talk to your children about their online experiences, ask them about the apps and games they enjoy, and discuss the potential dangers of the internet, such as cyberbullying, online predators, and exposure to inappropriate content.

By fostering open dialogue, you can build trust and ensure that your children feel comfortable coming to you with any concerns they may have.

Another key strategy is to set clear limits on screen time. While technology can be a valuable learning tool, excessive use can have negative consequences, such as sleep deprivation, social isolation, and attention problems.

Establish age-appropriate guidelines for screen time, and enforce them consistently. Make sure to include time for other activities, such as outdoor play, reading, and spending time with family and friends.

It's also important to be aware of the content your children are consuming online. Familiarize yourself with the age ratings and content descriptors of the games and apps they use, and utilize parental controls to restrict access to inappropriate content. Encourage your children to engage with educational and enriching content that can expand their knowledge and foster their creativity.

In addition to setting limits and monitoring content, it's crucial to teach your children responsible online behavior. Discuss the importance of protecting their personal information, avoiding interactions with strangers online, and being respectful to others in online communities. Teach them how to identify fake news and unreliable sources, and encourage them to think critically about the information they encounter online.

Another aspect of digital parenting that is often overlooked is the importance of modeling responsible tech use. Children learn by observing their parents, so it's important to be mindful of your own digital habits. Avoid using your phone during family meals, set aside time for tech-free activities, and demonstrate healthy boundaries with technology.

Technology can also be a powerful tool for family bonding. Consider playing video games together, watching educational videos, or using apps to collaborate on creative projects. By engaging with technology as a family, you can create shared experiences, foster communication, and strengthen your relationships.

It's important to remember that digital parenting is not a one-size-fits-all approach. Every family is unique, with different values, priorities, and challenges. It's essential to tailor your approach to your family's specific needs and to be flexible and adaptable as your children grow and their needs evolve.

The digital age presents both challenges and opportunities for families. By embracing technology with a mindful and intentional approach, we can harness its power to enrich our children's lives and prepare them for the future.

Digital parenting is not about control or restriction; it's about empowerment and education. It's about equipping our children with the skills and knowledge they need to navigate the digital world safely, responsibly, and creatively.

With open communication, clear boundaries, and a focus on responsible use, we can turn the challenges of the digital age into opportunities for growth, connection, and learning. Remember, you are not alone in this journey.

There are countless resources available to support parents in navigating the digital landscape. By staying informed, seeking guidance when needed, and adapting your approach as your children grow, you can create a digital environment that is both safe and enriching for your family.

ᐅᐅᐅ

"Digital parenting isn't about control; it's about connection. Let's navigate the digital landscape together, empowering our kids with the knowledge and confidence to thrive."

SEVEN

The Future is Now: Raising Kids Who Shape Tomorrow's Technology.

The relentless pace of technological advancement is transforming our world at an unprecedented rate. What was once considered science fiction is now a part of our daily lives, and the possibilities for the future seem limitless. In this dynamic landscape, our children are not merely passive observers; they are the architects of tomorrow's technology. As parents, educators, and mentors, we have a unique opportunity to empower them to shape this future, to become the innovators, creators, and leaders who will drive progress and solve the challenges of our time.

The future is not a distant concept; it's unfolding before our eyes. Artificial intelligence, robotics, biotechnology, and virtual reality are no longer futuristic buzzwords; they are tangible realities that are already impacting our lives. Our children are growing up in a world where technology is seamlessly integrated into every aspect of their existence. From the smartphones they use to communicate with their friends to the educational apps that help them learn and explore, technology is a constant companion. This ubiquity of technology presents both challenges and opportunities.

The challenge lies in ensuring that our children are not merely consumers of technology but active participants in its creation. It's easy to fall into the trap of simply handing our children the latest gadgets and allowing them to passively consume content. But this approach does a disservice to their potential. We must encourage them to go beyond consumption and embrace creation.

This means fostering a mindset of curiosity and exploration. We must encourage our children to ask questions, to experiment, to tinker, and to seek out new knowledge. We must provide them with the resources and opportunities to learn about different technologies, to try their hand at coding, to build robots, and to explore the possibilities of virtual reality. By nurturing their innate curiosity, we can spark a lifelong passion for learning and discovery.

Creativity is another essential ingredient in shaping tomorrow's technology. The ability to think outside the box, to imagine new possibilities, and to develop innovative solutions is what will set our children apart in the future. We must encourage them to embrace their creativity, to express themselves through technology, and to use their imagination to create something new.

Collaboration is equally important. The most groundbreaking technological advancements are often the result of collaborative efforts, bringing together diverse perspectives and skillsets. We must teach our children the value of teamwork, the importance of communication, and the power of collaboration. By encouraging them to work together on projects, we can help them develop the interpersonal skills they need to succeed in the future.

Of course, shaping tomorrow's technology is not just about technical skills. It's also about ethical considerations and social responsibility. We must teach our children to think critically about the impact of technology on society, to consider the ethical implications of their creations, and to use their skills for the greater good. By instilling a sense of social responsibility, we can ensure that our children use their technological prowess to create a better world for all.

The future is not predetermined; it's a blank canvas waiting to be filled. Our children have the power to shape this future, to create a world that is more connected, more sustainable, and more equitable. But they need our guidance and support. As parents, educators, and mentors, we must empower them with the knowledge, skills, and values they need to navigate the complexities of the digital age and to make a positive impact on the world.

This is not a task for the faint of heart. It requires a commitment to lifelong learning, a willingness to embrace change, and a belief in the power of our children to make a difference. But the rewards are immeasurable. By raising children who shape tomorrow's technology, we are not just preparing them for the future; we are building a brighter future for all.

ᐅᐅᐅ

"The future isn't a distant destination; it's happening now. Let's raise tech-savvy kids who aren't just prepared for the future, but actively shaping it."

EIGHT

Empower, Educate, Engage: Give Your Child a Head Start in Tech.

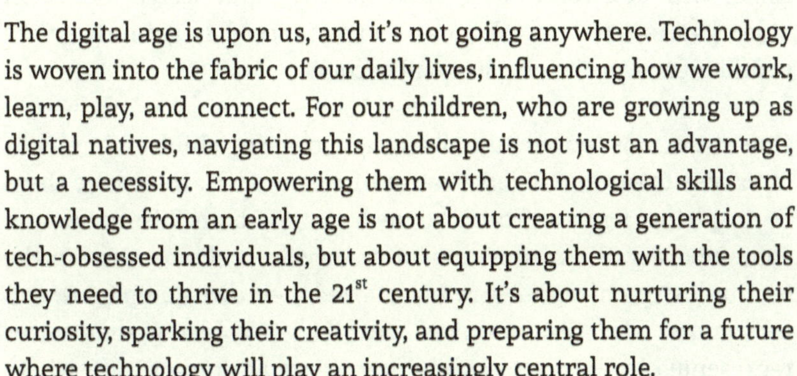

The digital age is upon us, and it's not going anywhere. Technology is woven into the fabric of our daily lives, influencing how we work, learn, play, and connect. For our children, who are growing up as digital natives, navigating this landscape is not just an advantage, but a necessity. Empowering them with technological skills and knowledge from an early age is not about creating a generation of tech-obsessed individuals, but about equipping them with the tools they need to thrive in the 21st century. It's about nurturing their curiosity, sparking their creativity, and preparing them for a future where technology will play an increasingly central role.

Empowerment begins with fostering a growth mindset. We need to instill in our children the belief that they can learn and master any technology, regardless of their initial skill level. This means praising their effort and perseverance, rather than focusing solely on their achievements. Encourage them to see challenges as opportunities for growth, and help them develop a resilient spirit that can withstand setbacks.

Education is the cornerstone of empowerment. It's not just about teaching children how to use specific tools or software; it's about fostering a deep understanding of how technology works. Introduce them to the basic concepts of coding, the principles of robotics, the intricacies of artificial intelligence, and the fundamentals of cybersecurity. Help them understand the impact of technology on society, both positive and negative, and encourage them to think critically about the ethical implications of technological advancements.

Engagement is key to making learning fun and effective. Children learn best when they are actively involved in the process. Provide them with opportunities to experiment, to build, to create, and to explore. Encourage them to participate in coding camps, robotics workshops, and online courses that cater to their interests. Let them tinker with electronics kits, build websites, and design their own video games. The more hands-on experience they gain, the more confident and proficient they will become.

One of the most powerful tools for empowering children in tech is to expose them to a diverse range of role models. Introduce them to inspiring figures from the tech world, both historical and contemporary. Share stories of women who broke barriers in the tech industry, entrepreneurs who started their own companies, and innovators who revolutionized our lives. By seeing themselves represented in these stories, children can envision a future where they too can achieve great things.

Mentorship can also play a crucial role in empowering children in tech. Connect them with mentors who can share their knowledge, expertise, and passion for technology. Mentors can provide guidance, support, and encouragement, helping children navigate challenges and discover their own unique path in the tech world.

It's also important to create a supportive and inclusive environment where children feel comfortable exploring their interests in technology. This means challenging stereotypes that suggest that certain technologies are "for boys" or "for girls." Encourage girls to embrace their inner techie, and boys to explore their creative side through technology. Create a space where all children feel valued and respected, regardless of their gender, race, or background.

As parents, we have a crucial role to play in empowering our children in tech. We can start by learning about technology ourselves, staying up-to-date on the latest trends and innovations. We can create a tech-friendly home environment, where children have access to age-appropriate devices and resources. We can encourage them to use technology responsibly and ethically, and we can be their biggest cheerleaders as they embark on their tech journey.

By empowering, educating, and engaging our children in tech, we are not just preparing them for future careers; we are equipping them with the skills and knowledge they need to be active participants in shaping the future. We are raising a generation of critical thinkers, problem solvers, and innovators who will tackle the challenges of tomorrow and build a better world for all. The future is now, and it's in the hands of our children.

ᚦᚦᚦ

"Empower. Educate. Engage. These aren't just buzzwords, but a roadmap to giving your child a head start in a world where tech literacy is the new literacy."

NINE

MORE THAN JUST GADGETS: NURTURING CRITICAL THINKING & DIGITAL SKILLS.

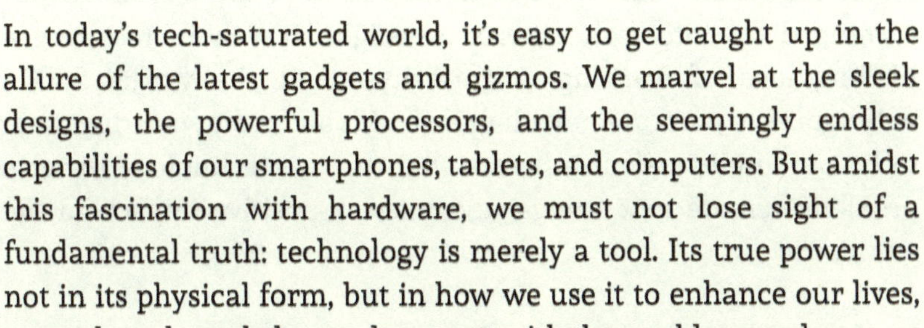

In today's tech-saturated world, it's easy to get caught up in the allure of the latest gadgets and gizmos. We marvel at the sleek designs, the powerful processors, and the seemingly endless capabilities of our smartphones, tablets, and computers. But amidst this fascination with hardware, we must not lose sight of a fundamental truth: technology is merely a tool. Its true power lies not in its physical form, but in how we use it to enhance our lives, expand our knowledge, and connect with the world around us.

For our children, who are growing up as digital natives, this distinction is especially important. They are surrounded by technology from a young age, and it's easy for them to become passive consumers, simply accepting the information and entertainment that is presented to them. But we have a responsibility to guide them towards a deeper understanding of technology, to help them develop the critical thinking and digital skills they need to become active participants in the digital age.

Critical thinking is the ability to analyze information, evaluate evidence, and draw logical conclusions. It's a skill that is essential for navigating the vast and often confusing landscape of the internet, where misinformation and disinformation abound. By teaching our children how to think critically about the information they encounter online, we can empower them to make informed decisions, avoid being swayed by false narratives, and develop their own unique perspectives.

Digital skills, on the other hand, encompass a wide range of abilities, from basic computer literacy to advanced programming. These skills are increasingly in demand in the workplace, and they are essential for success in many fields. By providing our children with opportunities to develop their digital skills, we can open up a world of possibilities for them, both personally and professionally.

Nurturing critical thinking and digital skills in children is not about turning them into tech experts overnight. It's about fostering a lifelong love of learning, a curiosity about the world, and a willingness to embrace new challenges. It's about empowering them to become independent thinkers who can use technology to solve problems, create new things, and make a positive impact on the world.

So, how can we achieve this? It starts with creating a home environment that encourages exploration and experimentation. Provide your children with access to age-appropriate technology, and encourage them to use it in creative ways. Let them build websites, design video games, or create digital art. Don't be afraid to let them make mistakes; learning often comes from trial and error.

As they explore, ask them questions that challenge their assumptions and encourage them to think deeper. Ask them why they believe certain information, how they would verify its accuracy, and what other perspectives might exist. Encourage them to question the status quo and to think critically about the world around them.

In addition to fostering critical thinking, it's important to provide children with opportunities to develop their digital skills. Enroll them in coding classes, robotics workshops, or online courses that teach them how to create websites, apps, or games. Introduce them to open-source software and encourage them to contribute to online projects. The more they learn and create, the more confident and capable they will become.

It's also important to be mindful of the content your children are consuming online. While there is a wealth of educational and enriching content available, there is also a lot of misinformation, disinformation, and harmful content. Teach your children how to evaluate sources, identify bias, and distinguish between fact and opinion. Encourage them to engage with diverse perspectives and to be respectful of others online.

Ultimately, nurturing critical thinking and digital skills is about more than just preparing children for the future workforce. It's about empowering them to become active and informed citizens who can use technology to make a positive impact on the world. It's about helping them develop the skills and knowledge they need to navigate the complexities of the digital age with confidence and integrity.

By investing in our children's critical thinking and digital skills, we are investing in a brighter future. We are raising a generation of innovators, problem solvers, and leaders who will shape the world for the better.

ppp

"Gadgets are just the beginning. Let's nurture our children's critical thinking and digital skills, turning them into responsible creators, not just passive consumers."

TEN

YOUNG MAKERS UNITE: HANDS-ON PROJECTS TO IGNITE A PASSION FOR TECH.

In a world increasingly dominated by digital screens and virtual experiences, there's a growing movement that seeks to reconnect children with the tangible joy of creation. The "Young Makers" movement is a celebration of hands-on learning, experimentation, and innovation. By engaging children in projects that require them to design, build, and tinker, we can ignite a passion for technology that goes beyond mere consumption and sparks a lifelong love of learning.

At the heart of the maker movement lies the belief that children learn best by doing. Rather than passively absorbing information, they thrive when they are actively involved in the learning process. Hands-on projects provide a unique opportunity for children to apply their knowledge, develop new skills, and unleash their creativity.

They learn to think critically, solve problems, and collaborate with others. These are essential skills for success in the 21st century, regardless of the career path they choose.

The beauty of maker projects is their versatility. They can be tailored to suit a wide range of interests and skill levels, from simple crafts to complex engineering challenges. The key is to choose projects that are both fun and challenging, that spark curiosity and encourage exploration.

For younger children, simple projects like building a cardboard robot or designing a marble run can be a great introduction to the world of making.

These projects allow them to explore basic concepts of engineering and design, while also developing their fine motor skills and creativity. As they grow older, they can tackle more complex projects, such as building a model rocket, designing a 3D-printed object, or coding a simple game.

One of the most exciting aspects of the maker movement is its emphasis on collaboration and community. Maker spaces, which are popping up in schools, libraries, and community centers around the world, provide a safe and supportive environment where children can come together to share ideas, learn from each other, and collaborate on projects.

These spaces foster a sense of belonging and empower children to take ownership of their learning.

The maker movement is not just about fun and games; it has real-world applications. Many of the skills that children develop through maker projects, such as problem-solving, critical thinking, and collaboration, are highly valued in the workplace. By nurturing these skills in our children, we are preparing them for the jobs of the future, many of which haven't even been invented yet.

The impact of the maker movement on children's lives is profound. It has been shown to increase their engagement in learning, improve their problem-solving skills, and boost their confidence. Children who participate in maker projects are more likely to pursue careers in STEM fields, and they are better equipped to adapt to the rapidly changing demands of the 21st-century workplace.

But the benefits of the maker movement go beyond academics and career preparation. It also fosters a sense of agency and empowerment in children. By allowing them to take ownership of their learning and create something tangible, we are sending a powerful message: their ideas matter, their creativity is valued, and they have the power to make a difference in the world.

In a world that is increasingly driven by technology, it's easy for children to feel overwhelmed and disconnected. The maker movement offers an antidote to this feeling.

By engaging in hands-on projects, children can develop a deeper understanding of technology, learn to harness its power, and create something meaningful. They can become not just consumers of technology, but creators, innovators, and problem solvers.

As parents, educators, and mentors, we have a responsibility to support the maker movement and encourage our children to participate in it.

We can start by providing them with the tools and resources they need, such as access to maker spaces, educational kits, and online tutorials. We can also create opportunities for them to showcase their creations, such as science fairs, maker festivals, and online communities.

But most importantly, we must foster a culture of creativity, experimentation, and collaboration. We must encourage our children to take risks, to embrace failure as a learning opportunity, and to work together to solve problems.

By doing so, we can ignite a passion for technology that will last a lifetime and empower our children to become the innovators and leaders of tomorrow.

ppp

"Young makers, unite! Let's transform garages and bedrooms into innovation labs, where hands-on projects spark a lifelong passion for tech."

ELEVEN

A Mom's Mission: Empowering Kids to Become Digital Creators.

As a mom navigating the digital age alongside my children, I've embarked on a personal mission. It's not about shielding them from technology, but about empowering them to become active participants in the digital landscape. I want them to be more than just consumers of content; I want them to be creators, innovators, and problem solvers who can harness the power of technology to express themselves, connect with others, and make a positive impact on the world.

This journey began with a simple observation: my children were spending an increasing amount of time on screens, passively consuming videos, games, and social media. While these activities had their place, I felt that there was a missed opportunity for them to engage with technology in a more meaningful way. I wanted them to discover the joy of creation, to see the digital world not just as a source of entertainment but as a canvas for their own ideas and imaginations.

This realization led me to embark on a quest to find ways to empower my children as digital creators. I started by introducing them to age-appropriate coding apps and games that taught them the basics of programming. We explored robotics kits that allowed them to build and program their own robots. We experimented with 3D printing, creating unique objects from their own designs. We even dabbled in video editing and animation, bringing their stories to life on screen.

The results were astounding. My children's eyes lit up with excitement as they discovered the power to create something from nothing. They became more engaged in their learning, more curious about the world around them, and more confident in their abilities. They were no longer just consuming content; they were creating it, and in the process, they were developing essential skills for the 21st century.

Empowering children to become digital creators is not just about teaching them technical skills. It's about nurturing their creativity, critical thinking, and problem-solving abilities. It's about helping them develop a growth mindset, where they see challenges as opportunities for learning and innovation. It's about fostering a love of learning that will last a lifetime.

As a mom, I've learned that empowering my children as digital creators doesn't require a degree in computer science or a deep understanding of complex algorithms. It simply requires a willingness to learn alongside them, to explore new technologies together, and to encourage their curiosity and creativity.

There are countless resources available to help parents on this journey. Libraries, museums, and community centers often offer workshops and classes on coding, robotics, and other tech-related topics. Online platforms like Khan Academy and Codecademy provide free tutorials and courses that children can access from home. And countless books and blogs offer tips and advice for parents who want to raise tech-savvy kids.

One of the most important things I've learned is that it's never too early to start. Even young children can begin to develop digital literacy skills by playing educational games, creating digital art, and exploring age-appropriate websites. As they get older, they can gradually progress to more complex projects and challenges.

The key is to make it fun and engaging. Let your children choose the projects that interest them most, and encourage them to experiment and explore. Celebrate their successes, no matter how small, and help them learn from their mistakes. Most importantly, create a safe and supportive environment where they feel free to express their creativity and take risks.

Empowering children to become digital creators is not just about preparing them for the future workforce. It's about giving them the tools they need to express themselves, connect with others, and make a positive impact on the world. It's about helping them develop the skills and confidence they need to thrive in the digital age.

As a mom, I believe that every child has the potential to be a digital creator. It's our job as parents to nurture that potential, to provide them with the resources and opportunities they need to succeed, and to celebrate their creativity and ingenuity. By empowering our children to become digital creators, we are not just preparing them for the future; we are shaping a brighter future for us all.

ϷϷϷ

"As moms, we have a mission. Let's empower our kids to embrace technology, not just as users, but as architects of a brighter, more inclusive digital future."

TWELVE

TECH FOR GOOD: RAISING KIDS WHO USE THEIR SKILLS TO MAKE A DIFFERENCE.

In our increasingly digitized world, technology has become a powerful force, shaping how we live, work, learn, and interact. While it offers immense potential for positive change, it's also important to recognize the potential for misuse and harm. As parents and mentors, we have a responsibility to guide our children towards using technology for good, to instill in them a sense of social responsibility, and to empower them to become agents of positive change.

The concept of "Tech for Good" encompasses a wide range of initiatives and activities that leverage technology to address social, environmental, and economic challenges. It's about using innovation and creativity to solve real-world problems, to create a more equitable and sustainable future for all. From developing apps that help people access healthcare to creating platforms that connect volunteers with those in need, the possibilities for Tech for Good are vast and inspiring.

Raising children who embrace this ethos starts with fostering a sense of empathy and compassion. We must teach them to see beyond their own experiences and to understand the needs and perspectives of others. Encourage them to ask questions, to seek out diverse viewpoints, and to challenge their own assumptions. Help them develop a deep understanding of the world's challenges, from poverty and inequality to climate change and social injustice.

Once children have a solid foundation of empathy and understanding, we can begin to introduce them to the concept of Tech for Good. Share stories of individuals and organizations who are using technology to make a difference, from young activists who are raising awareness about environmental issues to social entrepreneurs who are developing innovative solutions to poverty. Encourage them to explore these stories, to ask questions, and to think critically about how they can use their own skills and knowledge to contribute to the cause.

One of the most powerful ways to inspire children to use their tech skills for good is to provide them with opportunities to do so. Many organizations offer programs and initiatives that allow children to apply their technological knowledge to real-world problems. For example, they might participate in hackathons where they collaborate with others to develop solutions to social challenges, or they might volunteer their time to help organizations build websites or create educational content. These experiences not only provide valuable learning opportunities but also instill a sense of purpose and fulfillment.

Another way to foster a passion for Tech for Good is to encourage children to explore the intersection of technology and their own interests. If they are passionate about environmental issues, for example, they might research how technology can be used to monitor pollution levels or develop sustainable energy solutions. If they are interested in social justice, they might explore how technology can be used to empower marginalized communities or amplify voices that are often silenced. By connecting their passion with their tech skills, we can ignite a spark that can lead to lifelong commitment to social impact.

Of course, raising children who use their tech skills for good is not just about encouraging them to participate in specific projects or initiatives. It's also about instilling in them a set of values and principles that will guide their actions throughout their lives. Teach them the importance of ethics in technology, the need for diversity and inclusion in the tech industry, and the responsibility that comes with wielding powerful tools.

Encourage them to think critically about the potential consequences of their technological creations, both positive and negative. Help them understand the importance of data privacy, cybersecurity, and digital literacy. By equipping them with these essential skills and knowledge, we can empower them to become responsible and ethical users of technology.

The journey towards raising children who use their tech skills for good is an ongoing one. It requires a commitment to continuous learning, open communication, and a willingness to embrace new challenges. It also requires a belief in the power of young people to make a difference in the world. By nurturing their passion, fostering their creativity, and providing them with the tools and resources they need, we can empower them to become the next generation of Tech for Good leaders.

The future of our planet and our society depends on how we use technology. By raising children who are not only tech-savvy but also socially responsible, we can create a world where technology is a force for good, a tool that empowers us to solve problems, connect with others, and build a more just and equitable future for all.

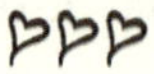

"Tech for good isn't just a slogan; it's a call to action. Let's raise kids who use their digital prowess to make a positive impact on the world."

THIRTEEN

Level Up Their Learning: Fun & Engaging Activities for Tech-Savvy Kids.

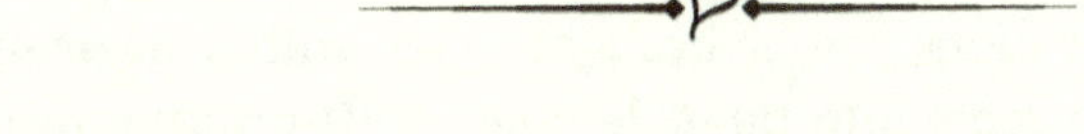

In today's digital age, children are growing up surrounded by technology. From smartphones and tablets to laptops and gaming consoles, screens are a ubiquitous part of their lives. While excessive screen time can be a concern, it's also important to recognize that technology can be a powerful tool for learning and development. By engaging children in fun and educational activities that leverage technology, we can help them "level up" their learning and develop valuable skills for the future.

One of the most exciting ways to engage tech-savvy kids is through coding and programming. Numerous online platforms and apps offer interactive coding courses for children of all ages. Scratch, for instance, allows kids to create animations, games, and stories using a visual block-based interface. Codecademy and Khan Academy offer more structured coding courses, teaching languages like Python and JavaScript in a gamified format. These platforms make coding fun and accessible, empowering kids to become creators of technology rather than mere consumers.

Robotics is another field that captivates young minds. Building and programming robots is a hands-on activity that combines creativity, problem-solving, and engineering skills. Various robotics kits are available, catering to different age groups and skill levels. LEGO Mindstorms is a popular choice for beginners, while Arduino and Raspberry Pi offer more advanced options for older children. Building robots not only teaches kids about electronics and mechanics but also nurtures their logical thinking and teamwork abilities.

For kids who love to tinker and build, 3D printing opens up a world of possibilities. They can design their own toys, gadgets, and even functional tools using 3D modeling software like Tinkercad. Once designed, these creations can be brought to life with a 3D printer, turning digital concepts into tangible objects. 3D printing fosters spatial reasoning, design thinking, and problem-solving skills, all while offering a satisfying sense of accomplishment.

The world of video game creation can be a captivating entry point into the world of technology for many kids. Platforms like Roblox and Unity provide user-friendly tools that allow children to create their own games, complete with characters, environments, and gameplay mechanics. This process teaches them about game design principles, programming logic, and storytelling, while nurturing their creativity and imagination.

For those with a creative flair, digital art and design offer endless opportunities for self-expression. Apps like Procreate and Adobe Illustrator allow children to create stunning illustrations, paintings, and graphic designs. They can even experiment with digital animation using tools like FlipaClip or Adobe Animate. These activities not only develop artistic skills but also introduce children to the world of digital media and design software.

Science and engineering enthusiasts can delve into the world of electronics and circuit building. Starter kits like Snap Circuits and littleBits offer a safe and easy way for children to experiment with electronic components and build simple circuits. As they gain confidence, they can explore more complex projects, such as building their own radios, alarms, or even robots. Electronics projects teach valuable lessons about electricity, circuits, and problem-solving.

Virtual and augmented reality (VR/AR) technologies offer immersive experiences that can enhance learning and creativity. Educational VR apps can transport children to historical landmarks, outer space, or the depths of the ocean, making learning more engaging and memorable. AR apps, on the other hand, can overlay digital information onto the real world, providing interactive experiences that blend the physical and digital realms.

Beyond these specific activities, there are numerous ways to incorporate technology into everyday learning. Educational apps like Duolingo and Khan Academy offer interactive lessons and quizzes in various subjects, making learning fun and accessible. Online platforms like Coursera and edX offer a vast array of courses for older children and teens, allowing them to explore their interests and learn new skills at their own pace.

In conclusion, the digital age offers a wealth of opportunities for tech-savvy kids to level up their learning and develop valuable skills for the future. By engaging in fun and educational activities like coding, robotics, 3D printing, game design, digital art, electronics, and VR/AR experiences, children can unleash their creativity, hone their problem-solving abilities, and gain a deeper understanding of technology. As parents and educators, it's our responsibility to guide and support them on this journey, ensuring that they use technology in a responsible and meaningful way. By doing so, we can empower them to become the innovators, creators, and leaders of tomorrow.

ᐅᐅᐅ

"Learning shouldn't feel like a chore; it should be an adventure. Let's level up our kids' education with fun and engaging tech experiences that ignite their curiosity."

FOURTEEN

Unlocking Creativity: Inspire Young Minds to Innovate with Technology.

In the heart of every child lies a wellspring of creativity, an innate capacity to imagine, invent, and express. Often, this creativity is stifled by traditional educational methods that prioritize rote learning and conformity over exploration and experimentation. However, technology, when harnessed thoughtfully, can be a powerful tool for unlocking this creativity and inspiring young minds to innovate. It's about moving beyond the mere consumption of digital content and empowering children to become active creators, problem solvers, and visionaries.

The digital age offers a vast array of tools and platforms that can spark imagination and fuel innovation. From coding platforms that allow children to create their own games and animations to 3D printers that turn their digital designs into tangible objects, technology provides endless possibilities for creative expression. But it's not just about the tools themselves; it's about how we use them to foster a creative mindset.

One of the most effective ways to inspire creativity is to encourage open-ended exploration. Give children the freedom to experiment with different technologies, to try new things, and to make mistakes. Don't be afraid to let them wander off the beaten path; sometimes the most innovative ideas come from unexpected places. Provide them with a safe and supportive environment where they feel comfortable taking risks and exploring their ideas without fear of judgment or failure.

Another key ingredient is collaboration. When children work together on creative projects, they learn from each other, share ideas, and build on each other's strengths. Collaborative projects also foster teamwork, communication, and problem-solving skills, which are essential for success in the 21st century. Encourage your children to participate in coding clubs, robotics teams, or maker spaces where they can collaborate with peers and mentors.

In addition to exploration and collaboration, it's important to provide children with inspiration. Introduce them to the work of artists, inventors, and entrepreneurs who have used technology to create amazing things. Share stories of how technology has been used to solve problems, improve lives, and change the world. By exposing children to the possibilities of technology, we can spark their imagination and inspire them to create their own innovations.

The role of technology in fostering creativity is not limited to digital tools and platforms. Even simple activities like playing video games can spark creativity. Games that encourage exploration, problem-solving, and world-building can stimulate children's imaginations and help them develop critical thinking skills. Encourage them to analyze the games they play, to think about how they could be improved, and even to design their own games.

Technology can also be a powerful tool for storytelling. Children can use digital tools to create animated videos, write and illustrate digital stories, or even compose their own music. These creative outlets allow them to express their emotions, share their experiences, and connect with others in meaningful ways.

As parents and educators, we have a crucial role to play in unlocking our children's creativity. We can start by creating a home and learning environment that values creativity and encourages experimentation. We can provide them with access to a variety of technological tools and resources, and we can encourage them to use these tools in creative ways. We can also provide them with opportunities to showcase their creations, whether it's through school projects, community events, or online platforms.

The future belongs to those who can think creatively and use technology to solve problems. By inspiring young minds to innovate with technology, we are not only preparing them for the jobs of the future but also empowering them to shape a better world. Let's unleash the creativity of our children and watch them soar.

ဝဝဝ

"Creativity isn't just for artists; it's the fuel of innovation. Let's inspire our kids to use technology as a canvas for their wildest ideas."

FIFTEEN

BUILDING A BRIGHTER FUTURE: ONE TECH-SAVVY KID AT A TIME.

The world is in a state of constant flux, driven by technological advancements that reshape our lives and redefine what's possible. The future, once a distant horizon, is rapidly approaching, and it's being shaped by the children of today. As we stand on the cusp of this new era, the importance of equipping our children with the tools and knowledge to navigate this ever-evolving landscape cannot be overstated. Building a brighter future, one tech-savvy kid at a time, is not just a lofty aspiration, but a critical mission that will determine the trajectory of our society.

This mission begins with recognizing that technology is not merely a collection of gadgets and gizmos, but a powerful force that can be harnessed for good. It has the potential to solve pressing global challenges, improve lives, and create a more equitable and sustainable world. But for this potential to be realized, we must empower our children to become not just consumers of technology, but creators, innovators, and problem solvers.

Empowering tech-savvy kids starts with fostering a love of learning and a curiosity about the world. We must encourage them to ask questions, to explore, to experiment, and to embrace challenges. This means providing them with opportunities to learn about different technologies, to tinker with electronics, to code, to build robots, and to explore the possibilities of virtual and augmented reality. It means creating a learning environment that is both fun and challenging, where children feel safe to take risks and learn from their mistakes.

Education plays a pivotal role in this process. We must equip our children with the digital literacy skills they need to navigate the online world safely and responsibly. This includes teaching them how to evaluate information critically, to distinguish between reliable and unreliable sources, and to protect themselves from online threats. We must also provide them with the technical skills they need to succeed in the digital age, such as coding, data analysis, and digital design.

But technical skills alone are not enough. We must also nurture their soft skills, such as communication, collaboration, and critical thinking. These skills are essential for success in any field, but they are especially important in the tech industry, where innovation often arises from the collision of diverse perspectives and ideas.

Mentorship is another key ingredient in building a brighter future. By connecting children with role models who can share their knowledge, expertise, and passion for technology, we can inspire them to pursue their own dreams and aspirations. Mentors can provide guidance, support, and encouragement, helping children navigate the challenges they may face and discover their own unique path in the tech world.

It's also important to create a supportive and inclusive environment where all children, regardless of their background or gender, feel empowered to explore their interest in technology. This means challenging stereotypes that suggest that certain technologies are "for boys" or "for girls." It means creating spaces where all children feel safe and welcome to learn, experiment, and create.

As we embark on this mission to build a brighter future, one tech-savvy kid at a time, we must remember that it's not just about individual success. It's about creating a generation of young people who are equipped to tackle the complex challenges of our time, from climate change and inequality to healthcare and education. It's about empowering them to use technology to make a positive impact on the world, to create solutions that benefit society as a whole.

The future is not something that happens to us; it's something we create. By investing in our children's education, nurturing their creativity, and empowering them to become tech-savvy, we are building a brighter future, one that is filled with hope, innovation, and possibility.

ᑭᑭᑭ

"Building a brighter future starts with one tech-savvy kid at a time. Let's equip them with the skills, knowledge, and values they need to make a difference."

SIXTEEN

The Digital Playbook: A Parent's Guide to Raising Tech-Confident Kids.

Raising children in the digital age can feel like a daunting task. Technology has become so intertwined with our lives that it's hard to imagine a world without it. But for parents, this new reality presents a unique set of challenges. How do we ensure our children are using technology safely and responsibly? How do we help them develop the skills they need to thrive in an increasingly digital world? And how do we strike a balance between embracing the benefits of technology and protecting our children from its potential harms?

This guide, "The Digital Playbook," aims to provide parents with a practical roadmap for navigating these challenges. It's not about creating rigid rules or banning technology altogether; it's about empowering parents with the knowledge and tools they need to raise tech-confident kids who can navigate the digital world with confidence, creativity, and critical thinking.

The first step in this journey is to embrace technology as a tool for learning and growth. Rather than viewing it as a distraction or a threat, recognize its potential to enrich your child's life. Technology can open up a world of information, connect your child with others, and foster creativity and innovation. By embracing technology as a positive force, you can set a positive tone for your child's relationship with it.

Next, it's important to establish clear boundaries and expectations around technology use. This means setting limits on screen time, creating tech-free zones in your home, and having open conversations with your child about responsible online behavior. It's also important to monitor your child's online activity, especially when they are young. This doesn't mean spying on them, but it does mean being aware of the websites they visit, the apps they use, and the people they interact with online.

Education is another key component of raising tech-confident kids. Teach your child about the potential dangers of the internet, such as cyberbullying, online predators, and exposure to inappropriate content. Help them develop the skills they need to protect themselves online, such as creating strong passwords, being cautious about sharing personal information, and avoiding clicking on suspicious links. It's also important to teach them how to be responsible digital citizens, such as respecting others online and avoiding cyberbullying.

In addition to safety and responsibility, it's important to help your child develop the technical skills they need to succeed in the digital age. This means teaching them how to use different devices and software, how to code, how to create digital content, and how to troubleshoot technical problems. These skills are not just valuable for future careers; they are essential for navigating everyday life in an increasingly digital world.

One of the most effective ways to foster tech confidence in your child is to engage with technology together. Play video games together, explore educational apps, create digital art, or build a website as a family. By sharing these experiences, you can not only bond with your child but also learn alongside them and model responsible tech use.

It's also important to encourage your child's creativity and curiosity. Technology can be a powerful tool for self-expression and exploration. Encourage your child to use it to create art, music, videos, or other forms of digital content. Help them discover their passions and interests, and support their exploration of new technologies and platforms.

Remember, raising tech-confident kids is not about being a tech expert yourself. It's about being willing to learn alongside your child, to embrace technology as a tool for growth and learning, and to create a safe and supportive environment where your child can explore the digital world with confidence and curiosity.

It's also important to remember that every child is different. What works for one child may not work for another. Be flexible and adaptable, and tailor your approach to your child's individual needs and interests. The most important thing is to foster a positive and healthy relationship with technology, one that empowers your child to learn, create, and thrive in the digital age.

ÞÞÞ

"The digital playbook isn't about rules; it's about empowerment. Let's guide our kids through the digital landscape, helping them become confident, responsible, and creative explorers."

SEVENTEEN

FROM CONSUMERS TO CREATORS: EMPOWERING THE NEXT GENERATION OF INNOVATORS.

In an era defined by rapid technological advancements, our children are immersed in a digital world from a young age. They are surrounded by screens, bombarded with information, and constantly exposed to new technologies. While this digital landscape offers numerous opportunities for learning and growth, it also poses a significant challenge: how do we empower our children to become not just passive consumers of technology, but active creators and innovators?

The traditional model of education, with its emphasis on rote learning and standardized testing, often stifles creativity and discourages experimentation. Children are taught to follow instructions, to reproduce existing knowledge, and to conform to established norms. While these skills are important, they are not enough to prepare them for a future that demands creativity, adaptability, and a willingness to embrace change.

To empower the next generation of innovators, we must shift our focus from consumption to creation. We must encourage our children to question, to explore, to experiment, and to express their unique ideas and perspectives. We must provide them with the tools, resources, and support they need to bring their ideas to life and to make a positive impact on the world.

This shift from consumers to creators is not just about learning to code or build robots, although these are certainly valuable skills. It's about fostering a mindset of curiosity, creativity, and resilience. It's about empowering children to see themselves as agents of change, capable of solving problems and making a difference.

One of the most effective ways to foster this mindset is to expose children to a wide range of creative activities and technologies. This could include anything from coding and robotics to music production, filmmaking, or even cooking. The key is to provide them with opportunities to explore their interests, to experiment with different tools and techniques, and to discover their own unique talents and passions.

It's also important to create a safe and supportive environment where children feel comfortable taking risks and making mistakes. Failure is an inevitable part of the creative process, and it's essential that children learn to embrace it as an opportunity for growth and learning. We must celebrate their efforts, encourage their experimentation, and provide them with the constructive feedback they need to improve.

Collaboration is another key ingredient in empowering the next generation of innovators. The most groundbreaking innovations often arise from the collaboration of diverse minds, each bringing their unique perspectives and skillsets to the table. We must encourage our children to work together, to share ideas, and to build on each other's strengths. This can be done through group projects, team challenges, or even simply by encouraging them to play and create together.

In addition to fostering creativity and collaboration, we must also equip our children with the technical skills they need to thrive in the digital age. This includes teaching them how to code, how to use design software, how to build websites, and how to navigate the vast landscape of online resources. But technical skills are not enough. We must also teach them how to think critically about technology, to understand its potential for both good and harm, and to use it in a responsible and ethical manner.

The journey from consumers to creators is not an easy one. It requires a significant shift in mindset, both for children and for the adults who support them. It requires us to challenge traditional notions of education and to embrace new approaches that prioritize creativity, collaboration, and problem-solving. But the rewards are immense.

By empowering our children to become creators, we are not just preparing them for the future workforce; we are equipping them with the skills and mindset they need to thrive in an ever-changing world. We are creating a generation of innovators who are not afraid to challenge the status quo, to think outside the box, and to use their talents to make a positive impact on the world.

ppp

"From consumers to creators, let's shift the paradigm. Let's empower the next generation to not just use technology, but to build it, shape it, and redefine it."

EIGHTEEN

THE POWER OF PLAY: LEARNING THROUGH FUN & EDUCATIONAL TECH EXPERIENCES.

In an era where technology is ubiquitous, it's easy to overlook its transformative potential in education. However, a growing body of research suggests that when harnessed effectively, technology can revolutionize the way children learn. This isn't about replacing traditional teaching methods but about augmenting them with engaging, interactive, and personalized experiences that cater to the digital natives of today. The key lies in recognizing the power of play and leveraging fun and educational tech experiences to foster a lifelong love of learning.

Play is not merely a frivolous pastime; it's a fundamental aspect of human development. Through play, children explore their world, experiment with new ideas, and develop essential cognitive, social, and emotional skills. In the digital age, technology offers a vast array of tools and platforms that can enhance and expand the possibilities of play, creating a rich and immersive learning environment.

Educational apps and games, for instance, can transform mundane subjects into exciting adventures. Math apps that turn equations into puzzles, language learning apps that gamify vocabulary acquisition, and science apps that simulate experiments can make learning fun and engaging. These experiences not only reinforce academic concepts but also cultivate critical thinking, problem-solving, and creativity.

Virtual and augmented reality (VR/AR) technologies offer another avenue for playful learning. VR headsets can transport children to historical landmarks, outer space, or the depths of the ocean, allowing them to experience these environments in a way that textbooks and videos simply cannot replicate. AR apps can overlay digital information onto the real world, creating interactive experiences that blend the physical and digital realms. These immersive technologies can spark curiosity, deepen understanding, and make learning a truly memorable experience.

Robotics and coding platforms also offer a unique blend of play and learning. Children can build and program their own robots, create animations and games, or design websites and apps. These hands-on experiences not only teach them valuable technical skills but also foster creativity, problem-solving, and logical thinking.

The power of play extends beyond individual learning. Online multiplayer games and collaborative platforms can foster social interaction, teamwork, and communication skills. Children can work together to solve puzzles, build virtual worlds, or create digital art. These experiences not only enhance their social and emotional development but also prepare them for the collaborative nature of the modern workplace.

It's important to note that not all screen time is created equal. Mindless consumption of videos or games can be detrimental to a child's development. The key is to choose educational tech experiences that are age-appropriate, engaging, and aligned with their interests. Look for apps and games that encourage active participation, problem-solving, and creativity.

Parents and educators play a crucial role in guiding children towards meaningful tech experiences. By setting limits on screen time, curating content, and engaging with children in their digital play, adults can help them maximize the educational benefits of technology while minimizing potential risks. It's also important to provide children with opportunities to balance their screen time with offline activities, such as outdoor play, reading, and spending time with family and friends.

The power of play in education is undeniable. By harnessing the fun and engaging nature of technology, we can transform learning from a chore into an adventure. We can create a generation of learners who are not only knowledgeable but also passionate, creative, and adaptable. We can empower them to become lifelong learners who are eager to explore the world and make their mark on it. The future of education lies in embracing the power of play and leveraging technology to create a more engaging, interactive, and personalized learning experience for all children.

"Play isn't just for fun; it's a powerful learning tool. Let's harness the power of play to create educational tech experiences that ignite a lifelong love of learning."

NINETEEN

A Parent's Toolkit: Essential Resources for Raising Digital Natives.

Raising children in the digital age can feel overwhelming, especially with the constantly evolving landscape of technology. But fear not, fellow parents! You are not alone in this journey. There is a wealth of resources available to help you navigate the complexities of the digital world and empower your children to thrive as digital natives. Think of this as your essential toolkit, equipped with the knowledge, tools, and support you need to raise tech-savvy, responsible, and resilient kids.

1. Educational Websites and Apps:

Common Sense Media: This invaluable resource offers age-appropriate reviews and ratings for movies, TV shows, games, apps, and websites. It also provides helpful tips and advice on digital parenting topics like screen time, online safety, and cyberbullying.

ConnectSafely: This organization provides research-based safety tips, parents' guidebooks, advice, news, and commentary on all aspects of tech use and raising digital natives.

Family Online Safety Institute (FOSI): FOSI is a global, non-profit organization that works to make the online world safer for kids and their families. Their website offers resources, tools, and research on a variety of digital parenting topics.

NetSmartz: This program from the National Center for Missing and Exploited Children (NCMEC) provides age-appropriate resources to help teach children how to be safer online with the goal of preventing child exploitation.

2. Online Courses and Workshops:

Parenting in a Digital World: This course offered by several universities and online platforms covers topics such as screen time management, online safety, cyberbullying, and digital citizenship.

Cyberwise: This non-profit organization offers online workshops and webinars for parents on topics like digital literacy, online privacy, and social media safety.

The Family Tech Agreement: This resource from Google helps families create a personalized agreement about technology use in their home, covering everything from screen time limits to online safety rules.

3. Books and Articles:

"The Art of Screen Time" by Anya Kamenetz: This book provides a balanced perspective on screen time, offering guidance on how to make the most of technology while also setting healthy limits.

"Glow Kids" by Nicholas Kardaras: This book explores the potential negative impacts of excessive screen time on children's brains and development.

"Screenwise" by Devorah Heitner: This book offers practical advice on how to raise kids who are tech-savvy and responsible online.

4. Community Resources:

Parent-Teacher Associations (PTAs): Many PTAs offer workshops and presentations on digital parenting topics, providing a space for parents to connect and learn from each other.

Local Libraries: Libraries often have resources on digital parenting, as well as technology classes and workshops for both children and adults.

Community Centers: Some community centers offer programs and activities that teach children digital skills, such as coding, robotics, and digital art.

5. Government Resources:

Federal Trade Commission (FTC): The FTC website offers resources for parents on protecting children's privacy online, avoiding scams, and dealing with identity theft.

Federal Communications Commission (FCC): The FCC website provides information on parental controls, internet safety, and digital literacy.

6. Technology Tools:

Parental Control Software: Tools like Net Nanny, Qustodio, and Bark can help parents monitor and manage their children's online activity.

Screen Time Management Apps: Apps like Screen Time, FamilyTime, and OurPact allow parents to set limits on screen time, schedule downtime, and block certain apps or websites.

Filtering and Blocking Software: Tools like OpenDNS and Norton Family Premier can help filter out inappropriate content and block access to certain websites.

7. Support Networks:

Online Parenting Forums and Groups: Connect with other parents who are facing similar challenges and share experiences, advice, and support.

Parenting Support Groups: Many communities offer in-person support groups where parents can discuss digital parenting issues and get advice from experts.

Therapists and Counselors: If you are concerned about your child's technology use or its impact on their mental health, consider seeking professional guidance from a therapist or counselor.

Raising digital natives is a journey, not a destination. It's about staying informed, being proactive, and adapting your approach as your child grows and the technology landscape evolves. By utilizing these essential resources, you can equip yourself with the knowledge, tools, and support you need to navigate this journey with confidence and raise tech-savvy kids who are prepared for the future. Remember, you are not alone in this endeavor. With the right resources and support, you can successfully guide your children through the digital world and empower them to thrive.

ᐅᐅᐅ

"Parents, you're not alone. Your digital toolkit is filled with resources, support, and guidance to help you raise tech-savvy kids who are ready to take on the world."

TWENTY

GIRL POWER IN TECH: INSPIRING YOUNG WOMEN TO EMBRACE THEIR INNER GEEK

In the vast and ever-evolving landscape of technology, a vibrant movement is gaining momentum: Girl Power in Tech. This isn't just a catchy phrase; it's a powerful call to action, an invitation for young women to embrace their inner geek and stake their claim in a field that has historically been dominated by men. This movement is about more than just increasing the number of women in tech; it's about fostering a culture of diversity, inclusivity, and empowerment that benefits everyone.

The tech industry is a driving force behind innovation and progress, shaping our world in countless ways. From developing life-saving medical technologies to creating platforms that connect people across the globe, the impact of tech is undeniable. Yet, for too long, women have been underrepresented in this field, their voices and perspectives marginalized. This not only limits the potential of women, but it also deprives the tech industry of the diverse talent and creativity that is essential for innovation.

Girl Power in Tech seeks to change this narrative by inspiring and empowering young women to pursue careers in technology. It's about breaking down stereotypes that suggest that tech is a "boy's club," and creating a welcoming and inclusive environment where girls feel supported and encouraged to explore their interests in STEM (Science, Technology, Engineering, and Math) fields.

This movement is multifaceted, encompassing a wide range of initiatives and strategies. It starts with education, providing girls with access to quality STEM education from a young age. This means not only teaching them the technical skills they need, but also fostering their curiosity, creativity, and problem-solving abilities. It means creating a learning environment where girls feel confident and empowered to take risks, experiment, and explore their interests without fear of judgment or failure.

Mentorship plays a crucial role in inspiring young women in tech. By connecting girls with successful women in the field, we can provide them with role models who can inspire and guide them on their journey. Mentors can offer valuable insights, advice, and support, helping girls navigate the challenges they may face and build the confidence they need to succeed.

Creating a supportive community is also essential. Online forums, social media groups, and in-person meetups can provide girls with a safe space to connect with other like-minded individuals, share their experiences, and learn from each other. These communities can foster a sense of belonging and empower girls to pursue their dreams in tech.

Another important aspect of the Girl Power in Tech movement is challenging stereotypes and biases. This means confronting the unconscious biases that can hold girls back, both in the classroom and in the workplace. It means celebrating the achievements of women in tech and highlighting their contributions to the field. It also means creating a culture where diversity is valued and everyone feels welcome and respected.

The impact of Girl Power in Tech is already being felt. More and more young women are pursuing degrees in computer science and engineering, and they are landing jobs at top tech companies. They are starting their own businesses, developing innovative products, and leading teams of talented engineers and designers. These women are not only breaking down barriers, but they are also changing the face of the tech industry, bringing new perspectives and ideas to the table.

But the work is far from over. There are still significant challenges to overcome. Women remain underrepresented in leadership positions in the tech industry, and they often face discrimination and harassment. We must continue to advocate for policies and practices that promote diversity and inclusion, and we must create a culture where everyone feels valued and respected.

The Girl Power in Tech movement is not just about women; it's about creating a better future for everyone. A diverse and inclusive tech industry is a more innovative and successful one. By empowering young women to embrace their inner geek, we are not only creating opportunities for them, but we are also building a stronger and more vibrant tech community that benefits us all.

ꔮꔮꔮ

"Girls, your inner geek is your superpower. Embrace it, nurture it, and let it propel you to the forefront of the tech revolution."

TWENTY-ONE

THE JOY OF LEARNING: IGNITE A LIFELONG PASSION FOR TECHNOLOGY IN YOUR CHILD.

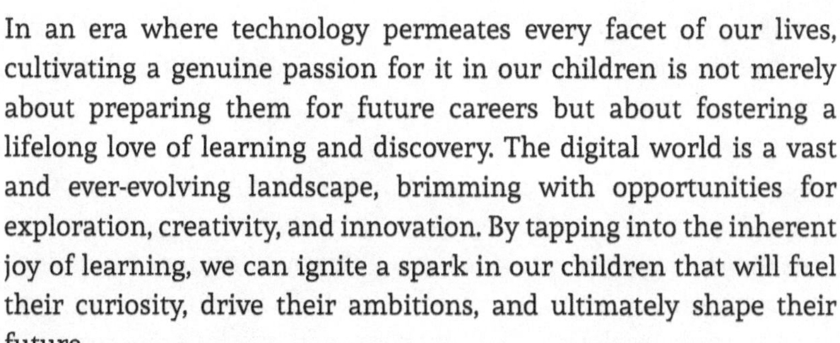

In an era where technology permeates every facet of our lives, cultivating a genuine passion for it in our children is not merely about preparing them for future careers but about fostering a lifelong love of learning and discovery. The digital world is a vast and ever-evolving landscape, brimming with opportunities for exploration, creativity, and innovation. By tapping into the inherent joy of learning, we can ignite a spark in our children that will fuel their curiosity, drive their ambitions, and ultimately shape their future.

At its core, the joy of learning is about intrinsic motivation. It's the thrill of discovering something new, the satisfaction of overcoming a challenge, and the excitement of sharing knowledge with others.

When children experience this joy, they become active participants in their own education, eager to explore, experiment, and expand their horizons.

In the context of technology, this joy can be found in a multitude of ways. It could be the excitement of building a robot from scratch, the satisfaction of coding a simple game, or the wonder of exploring virtual worlds through a VR headset. It could be the thrill of collaborating with others on a tech project, the pride of sharing a digital creation with the world, or the simple pleasure of learning something new about how technology works.

To ignite this passion in our children, we must first create an environment that encourages exploration and experimentation. This means providing them with access to a variety of technological tools and resources, such as computers, tablets, coding apps, robotics kits, and maker spaces. It also means giving them the freedom to explore these tools at their own pace, to try new things, and to make mistakes without fear of judgment or criticism.

We must also be mindful of the messages we send about technology. If we constantly portray it as a distraction or a threat, our children are likely to internalize these negative attitudes. Instead, we should emphasize the positive aspects of technology, highlighting its potential to empower, connect, and inspire.

One of the most effective ways to ignite a passion for technology is to make learning fun and engaging. This means incorporating play into the learning process, allowing children to explore technology through games, puzzles, and challenges. It also means finding ways to connect technology to their interests and passions. For example, if a child is interested in animals, they might enjoy using a nature app to identify different species or creating a digital presentation about their favorite animal.

We must also recognize that learning is not confined to the classroom. Technology can be a powerful tool for learning outside of school, whether it's through online courses, educational apps, or simply by exploring the vast resources available on the internet. By encouraging children to take ownership of their learning and to explore their interests independently, we can foster a lifelong love of learning that extends far beyond the school years.

The role of parents and educators in this process is crucial. We must be more than just providers of information; we must be facilitators of learning, guides who help children navigate the digital landscape, and mentors who inspire them to reach their full potential. This means being willing to learn alongside our children, to explore new technologies together, and to celebrate their successes and support them through their challenges.

Igniting a lifelong passion for technology in our children is not just about preparing them for future careers. It's about empowering them to become curious, creative, and critical thinkers who can use technology to solve problems, improve lives, and make a positive impact on the world. It's about nurturing a generation of innovators, entrepreneurs, and leaders who will shape the future of our society.

By embracing the power of play, fostering a love of learning, and providing our children with the tools and resources they need, we can ignite a spark that will burn brightly for a lifetime. We can empower them to become the architects of their own future, and in doing so, we can build a brighter future for us all.

ԹԹԹ

"The joy of learning isn't just about grades; it's about sparking a passion that lasts a lifetime. Let's ignite that spark in our kids and watch them illuminate the world with their brilliance."

TWENTY-TWO
SUMMARY

The digital age is an exhilarating and sometimes daunting frontier for parents raising children today. This guide, born from a mother's journey through the evolving tech landscape, seeks to illuminate a path towards empowering the next generation of digital pioneers. We've explored the multifaceted ways technology can enrich children's lives, emphasizing the importance of not merely consuming but creating with digital tools.

The journey begins with recognizing the inherent power of technology to inspire and educate. From coding to robotics, from 3D printing to game design, the opportunities for hands-on, creative learning are endless. We've delved into the transformative potential of screen time, advocating for a shift from passive consumption to active engagement, turning gaming into a gateway for coding exploration.

Parents play a crucial role in this process. By embracing the "digital playbook," we can guide our children towards responsible tech use, fostering open communication, setting healthy boundaries, and encouraging critical thinking. It's about more than just limiting screen time; it's about empowering kids to make informed decisions, develop digital literacy, and navigate the online world safely and confidently.

Education plays a pivotal role in equipping children for the future. We've emphasized the importance of providing a well-rounded tech education that goes beyond gadgets. It's about nurturing critical thinking, problem-solving skills, and a deep understanding of how technology works. By exposing children to diverse role models and mentors in the tech field, we can spark their imagination and inspire them to pursue their passions.

The "Code Like a Girl" movement has emerged as a powerful force for empowering young women in tech. By breaking down stereotypes, providing mentorship opportunities, and fostering a supportive community, we can encourage girls to embrace their inner geek and become the next generation of tech leaders.

But it's not just about individual success. Raising tech-savvy kids is about building a brighter future for us all. By instilling a sense of social responsibility and encouraging children to use their tech skills for good, we can empower them to become agents of positive change. We can nurture a generation that leverages technology to solve global challenges, create innovative solutions, and build a more equitable and sustainable world.

This journey is not without its challenges. The digital landscape can be a minefield of misinformation, cyberbullying, and inappropriate content. But by equipping ourselves with the right tools and resources, we can navigate these challenges and empower our children to thrive. We can teach them to be critical consumers of information, responsible digital citizens, and ethical users of technology.

The future is now, and it's being shaped by the children of today. By empowering them to become digital creators, innovators, and problem solvers, we are not just preparing them for the future workforce, but also for the challenges and opportunities that lie ahead. We are raising a generation that is not afraid to embrace new technologies, to challenge the status quo, and to use their skills and knowledge to make a positive impact on the world.

So, let's embrace this digital journey together. Let's empower our children to explore, create, and innovate. Let's teach them to use technology for good, to think critically, and to collaborate effectively. And let's celebrate their successes, big and small, as they pave the way for a brighter future for all.

ᎠᎠᎠ

Citation And References

This book represents the culmination of extensive research and meticulous analysis, incorporating a diverse range of sources, including numerous books, scholarly studies, and personal experiences. Additionally, I have scoured various websites to gather relevant information and data essential for the compilation of this work. I have taken every precaution to ensure the accuracy of the information presented and have diligently cited all sources to acknowledge their contributions.

Despite these efforts, the possibility of inadvertent errors remains. I deeply value the insights of my readers and appreciate any feedback that can help identify and rectify such inaccuracies. I encourage you to bring any discrepancies to my attention.

Your feedback is not only welcome but crucial, as it will aid in correcting current editions and enhancing the content of future ones. I am committed to maintaining the highest standards of accuracy and reliability in my work and thank you for your support and understanding.

Additionally, I firmly uphold the principle of freedom of speech and expression as guaranteed under Article 19(1)(a) of the Constitution of India, and I respect the diverse viewpoints and expressions of all readers.

▷▷▷

Other Books Of The Author

1. Empowering Minds: A Journey into Women's Self-Discovery and Power
2. The Dynamics of Motivation: Catalyzing Thought into Action
3. Meditation and Mental Well Being: The Path to Inner Peace and Clarity
4. The Psychology of Child Education: Nurturing Future Generations
5. Ethical Enlightenment: A Modern Guide to Living with Integrity
6. Voices of Empowerment: Stories of Women Rising Against Odds
7. Social Psychology in Everyday Life: Understanding Human Connections
8. The Essence of Motivational Speaking: Inspiring Change in Others
9. Balancing Acts: Women, Work, and the Will to Lead
10. Guiding with Grace: Raising Children with Compassion and Awareness
11. The Power of Positive Aging: Embracing Life After Fifty
12. Building Resilient Communities: Social Work in Action
13. The Ethical Educator: Principles for Teaching and Learning
14. From Insight to Impact: Social Psychology for a Better World
15. The Ethics of Empathy: A Guide to Ethical Living
16. The Science of Empowering the Self: Navigating Life's Challenges with Psychological Wisdom
17. The Mindful Conscious Leader: Meditation Techniques for Modern Management
18. Pioneering Spirit: Women's Pathways to Leadership and Empowerment
19. Feeling to Healing: The Role of Emotional Intelligence in Child Development
20. Transformative Talks and Words of Inspiration: Insights into Motivational Oratory

21. Green Ethics: A Path to Sustainable Living
22. Spiritual Integrity: Navigating Life with Moral Compassion
23. Clean Living, Clean Society: The Ethics of Cleanliness
24. Patriotic Spirits: Building a Nation on Positive Attitudes
25. Innovative Integrity & Vibrant Visions: The Ethical and Entrepreneurial Spirit of Gujarat
26. Youthful Visions, Endless Possibilities: Inspiring Ethics and Motivation in Children
27. Living Your Legacy: How to Motivate Others by Living Your Values
28. Secret of Healing Conversations: Ethical Practices in Counselling and Therapy
29. Creative Kindness: Crafting a Life of Compassion and Creativity
30. The Power of Appreciation: How Gratitude Can Transform Your Relationships
31. Bhagavad-Gita: Messages
32. Science of Art: The New Frontier of Fashion Modernism
33. Vivekananda's Virtues: A Blueprint for Modern Living
34. Empower Her: Navigating the Path to Women's Entrepreneurship
35. The Boundless Classroom: Innovations in Global Education
36. The Language of Leadership: Communicating with Authenticity and Impact
37. The Warrior's Mantra: Deciphering the Hanuman Chalisa
38. Echoes of Empathy: Transformative Stories of Social Service
39. Artful Living: Cultivating Creativity in Your Daily Routine
40. Finding Your Why: Discovering Your Passions and Charting Your Course
41. The Role of Social Media in Shaping Self-Esteem and Interpersonal Relationships among Adolescents
42. Karma's Tapestry: Weaving a Life of Selfless Service
43. Altruistic Alchemy: Transforming Lives Through Giving
44. The Blueprint of Pro-Activeness and Productivity: Crafting Habits for Success
45. The Simplicity with Grounded Wisdom: Embracing Authenticity

Bhajan

101. Pilgrimage of the Soul: Spiritual Journeys in India

❧❧❧

Contact

Dr. Minakshi Bansal
Social Activist
Ahmedabad, Gujarat, Bharat
minakshiindiag20@yahoo.com

ᐅᐅᐅ

|| LOKAHA SAMASTHAHA SUKHINO BHAVANTU ||